The Aesthetic Clinicians Skin Scanner Guide

By *Florence Barrett-Hill, ITEC, CIDESCO* dips
Director of Education, Pastiche Resources

CONTENTS

How to get the best from your skin scanner

This booklet has been written for skin and beauty professionals like yourself to assist you in getting the best from your skin scanner or other black light equipment.
The methods and techniques described within have been proven to yield exceptional results and increase diagnosis accuracy significantly.
They are the result of over 20 years of experience and research.

A money making tool

The skin scanner is a truly useful tool that with practice will allow you to examine the skin in a manner you have never experienced before.
It will be possible to the trained eye, to view the skin as a group of multi-layered colours, with different conditions and colours at distinct strata levels.

This ability to look "behind" or "through" the skin will reveal far more condition detail than simply examining the surface, and with the assistance of the detailed colour interpretations contained within, you will be able you to identify, analyse and diagnose a wide variety of skin conditions with far more accuracy and confidence.
Accurate skin analysis is the foundation of your business.
It is on this foundation that your success, image and professional credibility is built.
Accurate diagnosis will ultimately lead to successful treatments, with increased sales of take home care and professional salon treatments following.

The correct use of the skin scanner will not only assist you in your diagnosis, but will also help educate your clients, as they are also able to see the same skin conditions and imperfections as you do.

How do skin scanners and black light devices work?

Ultraviolet light is emitted (at a wavelength of approximately 365-380 nanometers) onto the skin of the client, and depending on the physiological factors present and chemical composition of the acid mantle, any subsequent fluorescence will be shown as a variety of colours from dark brown through reds, oranges, purples and yellows.
Each colour indicates a physiological or chemical state.

The science of using UV light to examine the skin is related to photochemistry and termed fluorescence spectroscopy. It is the same method more expensive image based skin diagnostic devices use to take UV photographs of various skin conditions.

ypes of black light equipment

Hand held woods lamp

There are a number of black light devices available; the most familiar would be the hand held woods lamp of earlier years.

Many clinics still have these, but the usage has waned over time because of the difficulties in making them work efficiently. Focusing onto the skin surface meant that the client often got bumped on the nose.

ight bleed was also another problem and even though one could create a curtain to hroud the unit and block out the light bleed, difficulties always seemed to arise.

 however you do have a hand held woods lamp, this booklet will still assist you in iagnosing the colours seen.

kin Scanner / scope

his is the most popular and often used type of black ght equipment. Because of the controlled light onditions and high output of UV light, these devices re perhaps the most practical of all black light evices. Although more user-friendly than the hand eld woods lamp, usage still wanes from being unable correctly decipher the information gained.

his booklet has been written specifically for this type f black light equipment.

Skin Scanning cameras

There are still a number of specialist devices using black light and either digital or Polaroid film technology.

While these are convenient, unfortunately the same mistakes of misinterpreting the information are made when using this equipment as with the older hand held woods lamp .

This booklet will enable you to diagnose more accurately the images developed and prevent you making the same mistakes that will result in misdiagnosis of the skin.

Before you use the scanner: The introduction

Always ask the client if you may have a closer look at their skin. This is common courtesy.
Explain to the client the equipment you will be using, showing the client the scanner, briefly explaining how it works and how it will enable you to assess and confirm specific skin conditions.

Potential client apprehensions

There may be a number of questions your client may need to have answered to avoid anxiety. The two most common apprehensions experienced are claustrophobic and ultra violet light concerns. If your client appears apprehensive about being in a small confined space, inquire discreetly if they suffer claustrophobia, as this knowledge will ensure you don't leave them in the scanner for too long. This type of client may be examined in short 2 or 3- minute sessions to avoid panic.
Make your client aware that it can be close and warm in the skin scanner, telling them you will try to keep your analysis to a maximum of 5 minutes to maintain their comfort. If you require longer examination time, do your examination in 3-4 minute steps with sufficient breaks in between as necessary. Always ask your client if they are comfortable.

The black light in skin scanners is in the UVA region. (340-400nm)

Safety

While "black lights" do produce light in the UV range, their spectrum is confined to the long wave UVA region. (340-400nm) Unlike UVB and UVC, which are responsible for the direct DNA damage that leads to skin cancer black light is limited to lower energy, longer waves and does not cause sunburn However, UVA is capable of causing damage to collagen fibres and destroying vitamin A in skin when in sufficient levels for extended periods of time.
The low energy levels of UVA emitted by the skin scanner, combined with the very short exposure time (3-4 minutes) during examination make the devices completely safe to use.

Analysis preparation

t is **imperative** that all make up or creams, sunscreens etc be removed before proceeding with the examination, as any substances covering the skin surface will reduce the ability to obtain a true indication of the colors displayed. Remember that any chemicals and pigments will alter the skin surface reading, so any attempt to **accurately** read the skin under these conditions will be a waste of time.

n the event of a skin being freshly cleaned, be prepared to view sebaceous secretion levels **below** that which would give a true indication of the prevailing conditions. If at all possible, clean the skin at least 30 minutes before you intend to examine it in the scanner, or ask the client to arrive un-cleansed and without makeup, moisturiser or sunscreens applied.

The Analysis Procedure

1. Turn the machine on first. **Never** turn machine on when the client has their head nside the scanner, as the flashing of the fluorescent starters can be quite frightening. The skin scanner has a fan inside for client comfort. Explain to the client this is the noise she can hear.

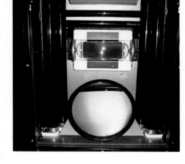

2. Ask your client to position their head in to the scanner, draping the hood around the back of the head and securing it with the Velcro tabs to reduce ight bleed. If the client is wearing white, cover with a dark coloured drape.

3. Ask client to adjust their position until they see their face in the small round mirror in the skin scanner. It will take a few seconds for their eyes to adjust to the lights within the enclosure.

Having ensured client comfort, move to the other side of scanner and adjust the eye piece to enable you to see the clients face clearly.

If the client wear glasses allow them to view their skin for a short time then ask for the glasses to be removed. This will then give you an unobstructed view of the eye area.

Give your own eyes time to adjust to different light conditions, then proceed with your analysis.

The Analysis Procedure

Important
When you first look at your client's skin you will see a plethora of colours, and in order to reduce confusion, it is recommended that one aspect of the skin is examined at a time.

The procedure on the following pages has proven both easy and accurate.

1. Ascertain the amount of undamaged skin

The first colours that will grab your attention will be the darker browns and redder purples, but as these are conditions, we will ignore them at this time.

Using a 3 dimensional field of viewing, look objectively behind all of the darker colours and ascertain the amount of lilac/cream (undamaged) skin on the facial area.

Use your reference colour chart to guide you.

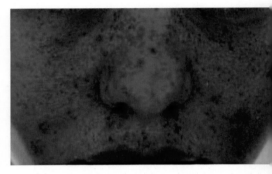

The first colours that will grab your attention will be the darker browns and redder purples, but as these are conditions, we will ignore them at this time.

Try to quantify this area of skin as a percentage. (i.e. 70% or almost 3/4 of the facial skin appearing lilac/cream in colour) Areas of lilac/cream skin may vary from less than 20% to 90% depending on majority skin type and conditions.

In many skins this colour can be faintly seen between the pigmentation and under eyebrows.

2. Ascertain key areas of thin skin density loss of structural integrity

There is always irregularity with most skins, the eye area is a naturally thinner skinned area and it is this area you can look to first to adjust your eyes to the colour you are looking for.

Closely associated with thin skin density is collagens loss of structural integrity.

If the thinner skinned areas have collagen loss, the scarlet tones displayed will tend to blend to burgundy shades as indicated on the colour chart.

You may have already ascertained areas of the face to have some vascular damage or diffused redness before using the scanner; as this condition is generally associated with thinner skinned areas, look to these areas next.

There you will find the varying shades of lilac/scarlet that will indicate to you the thinner density of the skin. The bridge to tip of the nose has most often been sun burnt at some time, so here you will usually notice a brighter more florescent lilac strip.

Using your face chart, mark the areas of thin skin density and collagens loss of structural integrity. If possible, try to quantify the percentage of these conditions.

3. Sebaceous secretions and flow rates

These will appear in varying shades of yellow, and be pin-pointed about the face. The T zone is a naturally occurring oily area, and this will be your first area to look at to accustom your eyes to the lipid colours. Again, do not rush and let the colour chart guide you. The various shades of yellow, melon to orange will indicate the viscosity of oil flow. A bright yellow indicates a free flowing sebaceous oil, and although it can be a problem to the client, it is not indicative of a skin condition. However, the melon to orange spots will indicate that the oil flow has become congested and sluggish. If the orange shade has a red/orange fluorescence overtone it will indicate porphyrins associated to the P acnes bacteria. Take note of the percentage and condition of oil flow and the areas where it was found.

4. Essential Fatty Acid Deficiency (lipid dryness)

If there is no apparent spots of oil in any areas of the T zone, you may be looking at a lipid dry skin. To confirm lipid dryness, bring your dimension of vision back to an overall view, and see if you can determine an aura of lilac to violet over the whole facial area.

If the aura is present, it will appear as a haze. Behind this haze is generally a lighter burgundy haze of thin skin density. This haze is often not visible in moderate levels of lipid dryness, however, if no yellow pin points are visible anywhere on the face, some degree of lipid dryness must be diagnosed.

5. Pigmentation

This next skin condition to look for will be apparent in varying shades of brown. Most pigmentation will be obvious without the use of a skin scanner, so note these areas before using the scanner and make those areas the first place to look to check the depth of pigmentation.

5. Pigmentation (continued)

Some pigmentation will look quite light in colour until inspected under the scanner. The depth of the damage will become evident by the intensity of brown shade.
Remember to ask your client to lift hair off their face so you can inspect the forehead and sides of cheeks. The temple, cheek, jaw-line, neck and forehead areas are particularly susceptible to sun damage, so take the time to check these areas carefully.

Childhood freckles that have faded with time will become apparent under the scanner, and there may be some initial difficulty in determining the difference between photo damage and the faded freckles.
To isolate the childhood freckles, look for areas of pigmentation that appear across the bridge of the nose, are small, similar in colour and of regular size.

Any other pigmentation outside of these parameters may be considered photo damaged, or pigmented skin conditions aggravated by hormonal, trauma or chemical causes.

6. Loss of pigmentation

On most skins, there are usually some areas with a loss of pigment due to any number of causes which may include physical injury, sun damage or bio-chemical effects, these being evident as whitened areas or spots.
Most surface scars are readily identified by normal visual inspection, however, some underlying scarring will be only be revealed under the skin scanner. Other areas that may also show as whitened are areas that have undergone dermabrasion treatment.

Reading the colour guides

Each of the colour guides features visual indicator data followed by a number of causes in order of severity denoted by

Thin Skin Density & Loss of Structural Integrity

ntify the visual indicators of loss of structural integrity around the eyes first, looking for small vertical es, and then look for diffused redness on cheeks & chin. Then check tissue strength/density by using the n scanner looking at the eye area first and then the cheeks.

Visual Indicators: Dark Maroon to burgundy shades across the eye-lid & around general eye area.
(a) Indication that fascia septa deterioration would be in the reticular layer and maybe subcutaneous/lower.
(b) Severe loss of supporting collagen fibril which has caused loss of dermal junction, rete` pegs and papillary layer.
(c) Loss of structural integrity due to Collagenase Enzyme.

Visual Indicators: Medium burgundy to lighter burgundy/ lilac shades across the eye-lid and around general eye area, cheeks, chin, strip down top of nose.
(a) Fascia septa deterioration upper reticular.
(b) Moderate loss of rete pegs and papillary layer.
(c) Loss of supporting collagen fibril around micro-capillaries.
(d) Loss of collagen integrity due to Collagenase Enzyme.

Visual Indicators: Lighter burgundy/lilac shades close to lash-line. Cheeks, chin, strip on top of nose / Peri oral. Scar tissue will also show this colour.
(a) A less serious degree of thin skin density.
(b) Early indication of collagenase activity.
(c) Loosing supporting collagen fibril around micro capillaries.

Visual Indicators: Lilac shades will vary across the facial area. Darker where there is visual diffused redness like the upper cheeks and chin.
(a) Collagen fibril has strength and the rete pegs and papillary layer have good density & rete` ridges.

Visual Indicators: Lilac shades that blend to almost no colour. This may be apparent under the eyebrows, and in the background between childhood freckles, and on a child's skin.
(a) Generally an indication of undamaged skin.

Sebaceous Gland Secretions

Sebaceous secretions are easily indicated by a skin scanner, majority rules so if there is an extensive amount of melon or yellow pinpoints it will also help you decide the basic majority skin type. Begin by looking at the T zone first, this is where the majority of sebaceous gland are found. Then check the outer areas of the face, under zygomatic and sides of the neck.

Visual Indicators: Fluorescence Red to Hot Orange pinpoints through the T zone, temple, under cheekbone. Open & closed comedones
(a) P acnes Porphyrins.
(b) High percentage of Free Fatty Acids.
(c) Cellular waste within sebaceous gland.
(d) Hyper-keratinisation. *(e)* Viscous oil flow.

Visual Indicators: Melon pinpoints around nose wings, cleft of chin or temple area or closed comedones.
(a) Free Fatty Acids.
(b) Cellular waste within sebaceous gland.
(c) Hyper keratinisation.
(d) Viscous oil flow.

Visual Indicators: Pink to melon pinpoints round nose wings, cleft of chin or temple area.
(a) Cellular waste within sebaceous gland.
(b) Hyper-keratinisation.
(c) Less viscous oil flow.

Visual Indicators: Deeper yellow pinpoints through T-zone, general face area, neck, décolleté.
(a) Free flowing sebaceous oil secretion, with minor viscosity problems.
(b) If only in the T zone it is not a majority, but may concern client.

Visual Indicators: Bright yellow pinpoints through T-zone, general face area, neck ,décolleté.
(a) Free flowing sebaceous oil secretion that is generally less viscou
(b) Take note of majority and areas before finalising analysis.

11

Lipid Dry or Essential Fatty Acid Deficiency

f there is no indication of sebaceous secretion, this skin is intrinsically lipid dry or has been made lipid dry by excessive use of cleansers. The skin may have Essential Fatty Acid Deficiency, and this would be indicated by nutrition or cellular age. If the shading is very light you are looking at the undamaged skin of a younger skin.

Visual Indicators: Extensive blue gray haze will indicate intrinsic lipid dryness and essential fatty acid deficiency. No yellow or orange pinpoints of sebaceous lipid anywhere on the face. May have lighter burgundy/lilac undertone of thin skin density on the cheek areas.
(a) Cellular Senescence of sebocyte. *(b)* Severe Essential Fatty Acid Deficiency. *(c)* Atrophy of sebaceous gland.

Visual Indicators: Blue gray haze some scattered yellow or orange pinpoints of sebaceous secretion around nose wings and cleft of chin and temples.
(a) Essential Fatty Acid Deficiency. *(b)* Atrophy of sebaceous gland. *(c)* Intrinsically lipid dry. *(d)* Lipid Peroxidation.
(e) Wrong skin care protocols have stripped acid mantle.

Visual Indicators: Blue/gray haze with undertone of light maroon.
(a) Lesser degree of EFAD with Underlying Vascular Damage
(b) Intrinsically lipid dry.
(c) Lipid Peroxidation.
(d) Atrophy of sebaceous gland.
(e) Wrong skin care protocols have stripped acid mantle.

Visual Indicators: Light lilac to cream lilac haze over a wide area of the face.
(a) Younger skin with a lesser degree of intrinsic lipid dryness.
(b) Minimal Essential Fatty Acid Deficiency.
(c) Early indication of Lipid Peroxidation.

Visual Indicators: Cream lilac haze over majority of face. Very little indication of underlying damage of other skin conditions normally seen under black light.
(a) Minor lipid dry haze and may be showing on the outer areas of the face and neck.
(b) Undamaged skin.

Pigmentation

Where the pigment is showing on the face is an indication of the effect UVR has had on the melanocyte, and the extent of cellular damage. So take time to identify where the pigmentation is before using the skin scanner. Photo types 4, 5 and 6 will show darker indications of the shades shown below.

Visual Indicators: Very dark purple with maroon overtones. Often seen without scanner but not always, on photo-types 5 & 6 this pigment may look very dark purple to Maroon under scanner. Seen with scarring. *(a)* Cellular Senescence. *(b)* Mitochondria DNA damage to melanocyte. *(c)* Loss of dermal epidermal junction, causing pigment granule to become part dermis.

Visual Indicators: Dark purple with maroon overtones in butterfly pattern. Fainter outline can be seen without scanner along zygomatic & upper-lip area. *(a)* Chemical stimulation of pituitary gland. *(b)* Melanin stimulating hormone cascade. *(c)* Build up of melanin granules in dermal-epidermal junction from MSH cascade. *(d)* Mitochondria DNA damage to melanocyte.

Visual Indicators: Mid purple with maroon overtones. Most often seen around hairline, back of hands as solar lentigines. Pigmentation is seen on the face without a scanner. *(a)* Cellular Senescence. *(b)* Mitochondria DNA damage of melanocyte. *(c)* Extensive sun exposure history. *(d)* Poor quality spinosum layer. *(e)* Damage to melanocyte dendrite. (shortened or lengthened). *(f)* Irregular placement of pigment granule in spinosum layer.

Visual Indicators: Dark softer maroon small & regular pigmented lesion, (ephelides/freckles) not visible without scanner. Seen across nose, cheeks and forehead. Genetics may have red undertone of Pheomelanin pigment (MC1R).
(a) Genetic nesting of melanocytes. *(b)* MC1R gene raises risk for skin cancer. *(c)* High risk for Mitochondria DNA damage.

Visual Indicators: Very dark brown to lighter brown pigmented lesions. (ephelides/freckles, moles and birthmarks) Visible without the scanner. Often a visible indication of other pigmented anomalies that will be seen with the scanner. *(a)* Genetic nesting of melanocytes with MC1R gene. *(b)* Mitochondria DNA damage. *(c)* Poor quality spinosum layer. *(d)* Damage to melanocyte dendrite. (shortened or lengthened).

Recording the examination

To keep a record of the examination, it is recommended that a face chart such as the example below be used to highlight areas of specific interest and to use as a referral or post treatment comparison. A master blank examination sheet that can be copied for use in the clinic is on pages 19 and 20 of this booklet.

Note that the various conditions have been graded in severity by numbers. These numbers are relative to the colours displayed in the appropriate colour identification chart in the center of this booklet.

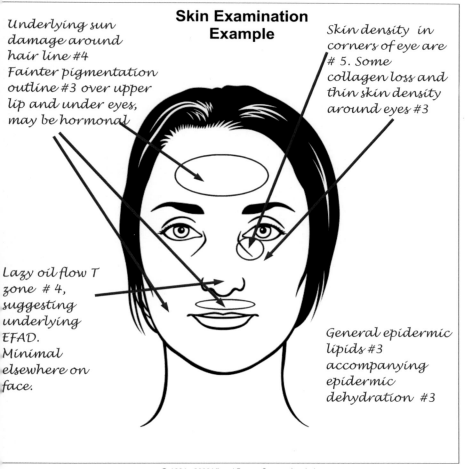

Skin Examination Example

Underlying sun damage around hair line #4 Fainter pigmentation outline #3 over upper lip and under eyes, may be hormonal

Skin density in corners of eye are # 5. Some collagen loss and thin skin density around eyes #3

Lazy oil flow T zone # 4, suggesting underlying EFAD. Minimal elsewhere on face.

General epidermic lipids #3 accompanying epidermic dehydration #3

Integrating the skin scanner in to a skin analysis

A true analysis of the skin can only begin when the therapist or practitioner understands the fundamentals of how each type and prevailing condition is recognised. In order to obtain a accurate picture of skin condition, you will use your knowledge of the structure and function of the skin. In addition, you will need to draw on the valuable resources supplied by your clients. (i.e. client skin history, diet, medical details etc.)

The skin scanner is one of a number of analysis tools that can be incorporated in to a professional skin analysis, and along with devices that measure the amount of sebum, hydration and melanin density, a great deal about skin health and conditions can be determined.

The skin scanner is particularly useful to determine areas of "invisible" pigmentation and the quality of sebum flow, however quantification of exact levels can only be achieved with measuring devices such as a Mexameter (pigment), Sebumeter, (sebum or oil) and Corneometer (hydration). The skin scanner is a vital tool as it shows where the areas of concern are and consequently where to conduct the measurements.

Where to look:

This same technique can be used with both normal visual (daylight or maggie light) and black light (skin scanner) examinations.

By dividing the facial area in to six principle zones, the examination can be made and recorded with more ease and accuracy.

The six zones are indicated at right. The benefit of breaking up the face in to the six zones allows more accurate "mapping" of areas of concern or interest.

The quantity and size of pores in these zones vary, and so what could be normal in one zone may be abnormal in another.

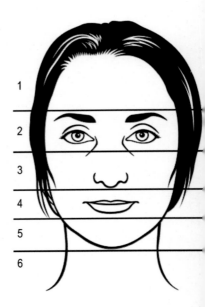

The Basic Majority Skin Type

In order to gain the most accurate results from your examination, it is essential that only one aspect of the examination be conducted at a time. The decision on what treatments are required is made only after all the facts are known.
The first phase of the procedure must be to determine the Basic Majority Skin Type. Only when the majority skin type is known, can prevailing conditions and finally disorders be diagnosed. Any attempt to analyse the skin in any other sequence will ultimately cause confusion, as priority of condition is of vital importance to the success of any treatments.

As the name implies, the majority must be the sum of what you observe most of in all the zones of the facial, neck and décolleté area. If a particular characteristic is present in most of the six zones, then it must be considered a majority.
Starting in zone one, work your way through to zone six, looking and noting down what is seen in each area, using the basic distinctive characteristics of skin texture, skin colour and observed secretions as your guide.

Some skin analysis tips

If there are characteristics that the client may be able to provide some information about, ASK! Always ask questions using the questioning key words, like what, why, when, where and how to help provide data about any anomalies you may see.
The client can usually provide a wealth of information.

GOLDEN RULE: Always think about the cause of the conditions you see, not how you would treat it.

How to look

The contemporary method of viewing the skin is somewhat different than what you may have practiced in the past.
A good light source is of paramount importance. Strong natural light or a maggie light with daylight tubes will give the best results. Avoid soft white tubes, as they give inaccurate colour perception. For inspection of details a pair of magnifying glasses may assist you in identification.

Always use a light source behind the area being analysed, and observe the following:

- Always keep client in an upright position. (Remember gravity)
- Do not look directly down on to the skin, always look across the skin.
- Use a **3 dimensional** type of viewing, that is look at the surface, its characteristics and then look directly behind the surface. The skin is not a solid colour but appears quite opaque. Look at the colours, textures and secretions and think about what has caused what you see.
- Try to think **behind** the surface.

When to use the skin scanner

It is after a normal (daylight or maggie lamp) examination that you should use the skin scanner. There will usually be areas of interest noted under normal full spectrum light that you will want to compare under black light.
It is not uncommon to re-examine areas of interest revealed by the black light under normal light for comparison, for example the burgundy areas of loss of structural integrity under black light will usually reveal tell-tale tiny vertical lines when viewed under normal light sources.

Using the same comparison technique, oily skins that reveal bright yellow pinpoints of free-flowing sebaceous flow, generally appears quite shiny under normal lighting conditions, and in many cases evidence of underlying diffused redness due to over treatment with harsh oil-removing skin care products.

Important note for pigmentation diagnosis

It is important to understand that when using the skin scanner to diagnose pigmentation problems, it is unwise to use it as a comparative "before and after" treatment indicator. This is because in most cases pigmentation treatments do not **totally** remove the pigmentation, and it will always still be evident under black light although not visible under normal lighting conditions.
It should be used only to diagnose conditions and demonstrate to the client where the damage is and to what depth it reaches.
It is unrealistic to demonstrate how well a pigmentation treatment works by examining under black light post treatment.

Skin analysis tips

Determining Basic Majority Skin Types

No two skins are exactly alike, but most have a combination of characteristics which enable them to be categorised according to a specific type.

Realistically, only three basic skin types exist, and any variations outside the basic type framework should be considered conditions within the basic type.

The three basic types are categorised lipid dry, oily and permanent diffused redness. (Also known as sensitive)
These three majority skin types are the basis on which your final analysis will be built , and must be correct in order for any subsequent treatment programs to have any long term effect.

You will note that the terminology **normal** and **combination** skins are not used in this manual. These are now considered inaccurate and unrealistic terms contrived for the non-specific domestic retail market over 30 years ago. For the sake of your credibility, do not use them with your clients. Be specific and professional at all times.

Three basic skin types:

- **Lipid (oil) dry**
- **Permanent diffused redness**
- **Oily**

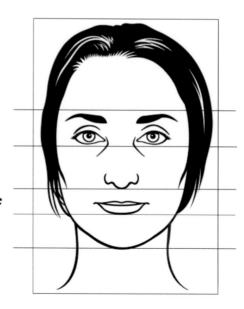

The three basic skin types are **intrinsic,** and this means you are born with a pre-disposition towards one of these three.
All other skin abnormalities are **extrinsic** or developed through work/play lifestyle and called **a skin condition**.

Skin Scanner Examination

Client name: ....

Consulted by: ....….Date: ....

General comments/observations: ....

....

....

....

Skin Scanner Examination

Client name: ....

Consulted by: ....Date: ....

General comments/observations: ....

....

....

....

About the author of *Scanning Secrets*

New Zealand born **Florence Barrett-Hill** is an internationally acclaimed independent dermal scientist, aesthetic technical educator, practitioner, researcher, and author with a vast experience covering all aspects of professional aesthetic therapy and paramedical skin care. Florence holds over a dozen diplomas and international qualifications covering every aspect of modern skin treatment therapy, and is well respected by her industry peers for her 30+ years of knowledge she loves to share.

Florence's internationally respected "Advanced Skin Analysis" training program is a breakthrough post-graduate curriculum launched in 1994, and was the first to recognise and teach the importance of linking skin  structure and function to skin condition. It is the core of this training program that has provided the content for the book of the same name, first published in 2004.

Many leading icons in professional skin care recognise Florence as one of the few people uniquely capable to take beauty therapy and aesthetics in to the realms of scientific skin care, with her expertise sought by organisations internationally. Many graduates and peers truly believe she provides the most informative and effective schooling for skin treatment practitioners and beauty therapists in the world.

Other titles by Florence Barrett-Hill

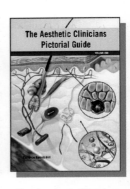

Advanced Skin Analysis	Cosmetic Chemistry	The Aesthetic Clinicians
ISBN 978-0-476-00665-2	ISBN 978-0-473-12467-0	Pictorial Guide

Available from the bookstore or supplier of this publication